CONTENTS

LUCKY LUCIANO

INTRODUCTION

C harles "Lucky" Luciano is one of the most infamous and enigmatic figures in the history of organized crime. Born Salvatore Lucania in Sicily in 1897, Luciano rose from humble beginnings as an immigrant in New York City to become one of the most powerful and influential crime bosses in American history.

Luciano's life was marked by a series of unlikely twists and turns, from his early involvement in street gangs to his role in the creation of the Five Families and the establishment of the Commission, a governing body for organized crime in the United States. He was a crucial figure in the Prohibition-era bootlegging and speakeasy scene, working with other notorious crime bosses like Al Capone and Meyer Lansky.

Despite his criminal activities, Luciano was also known for his charm and savvy business acumen. He was a master of strategy and negotiation, and his ability to form alliances and broker deals with other crime bosses was a key factor in his success.

However, Luciano's reign was not without its challenges. He faced numerous attempts on his life, and he was eventually arrested and imprisoned on charges of prostitution. His eventual release and deportation to Italy marked the end of his direct involvement in the American underworld, but his influence continued to be felt for years.

Today, Luciano remains a legendary figure in American history, with a lasting legacy that extends far beyond the world of organized crime. He has been the subject of numerous books, films, and television shows, and his story continues to fascinate and captivate audiences around the world.

This book aims to delve deeper into the life and legacy of Lucky Luciano, exploring his rise to power, his involvement in Prohibition-era bootlegging and speakeasies, his eventual arrest and imprisonment, and his ongoing influence on the American underworld. Through interviews, historical research, and analysis of primary sources, we hope to shed new light on this complex and fascinating figure and offer a fresh perspective on the history of organized crime in America.

BIRTH AND EARLY LIFE

Salvatore Lucania, later known as Lucky Luciano, was born on November 24, 1897, in the town of Lercara Friddi, located in the rugged hills of Sicily, Italy. His parents, Antonio Lucania, and Rosalia Capporelli were the proud parents of five children, including Bartolomeo (born 1890), Giuseppe (born 1898), Filippa (born 1901), and Concetta. Antonio Lucania supported his family by working in a sulfur mine in Sicily, a laborious and dangerous job that provided little in the way of financial security.

While The Last Testament of Lucky Luciano: The Mafia Story in His Own Words has been widely considered as a reliable source, there are several issues that suggest it may not be entirely truthful. According to The New York Times, the book is based on conversations that Luciano allegedly had with Hollywood producer Martin Gosch in the years leading up to his death. However, the book quotes Luciano discussing events that took place long after his passing, regurgitates factual errors from prior Mafia literature, and details Luciano's involvement in meetings that took place while he was incarcerated. These concerns have led some to question the authenticity of the book and to view it as potentially fraudulent.

In April of 1906, eight-year-old Luciano and his family left Sicily and made the journey to the United States, settling in the bustling city of New York. They established themselves in the Lower East Side of Manhattan, which was a popular area for Italian immigrants at the time. When Luciano was 14, he abandoned his studies and took up a job delivering hats, which paid $7 per week. However, after a lucky win of $244 in a dice game, Luciano left his job and began making money on the streets. In that same year, Luciano's parents enrolled him in the Brooklyn Truancy School to address his frequent absences from school.

As a teenager, Luciano broke off from other street gangs and established his own gang. He also joined the notorious Five Points Gang, which was infamous for its criminal activities. However, unlike other gangs that primarily focused on petty crimes, Luciano's gang offered protection services to Jewish youth who were targeted by Italian and Irish gangs. For a fee of just 10 cents per week, Luciano and his associates provided safety and security to those in need. During this time, Luciano also gained experience in the pimping trade, which was a lucrative industry in the years surrounding World War I.

It was during these early years that Luciano crossed paths with Meyer Lansky, a young man whom Luciano initially attempted to extort for protection money on his way home from school. However, Luciano was impressed by Lansky's bold and defiant response to his threats, and the two formed a close and long-lasting partnership.

The origins of Luciano's nickname "Lucky" are somewhat shrouded in mystery. It is unclear whether the moniker was earned due to his gambling prowess, or as a result of surviving a brutal attack in 1929. After refusing to work for another mob boss, Luciano was assaulted and had his throat slashed by three men, but managed to survive. It's also possible that the nickname simply stemmed from a mispronunciation of his last name, or a variation of it. Throughout his life, Luciano had numerous run-ins with the law, having been arrested a total of 25 times between 1916 and 1936 on charges ranging from assault to illegal gambling, blackmail, and robbery. Despite these repeated arrests, Luciano never served any time in prison. Interestingly, it's unclear how his surname came to be commonly spelled as "Luciano." Some have suggested that persistent misspellings by newspapers may have contributed to the change.

With a fierce determination to build a reputation for himself in the world of organized crime, Luciano made the decision to Americanize his name. His birth name, "Salvatore," was often shortened to "Sally," a nickname that had feminine connotations that Luciano sought to avoid. To overcome this, he opted to use "Charles" instead, which he felt was a more masculine name that better suited his aspirations. In time, even his last name was changed, with "Lucania" being transformed into "Luciano." With this new identity, Charles Luciano was born, a self-made man who was determined to climb to the top of the criminal underworld.

PROHIBITION

Starting on January 17, 1920, the Eighteenth Amendment of the United States Constitution was enforced, resulting in Prohibition, which lasted until its repeal in 1933. The amendment's implementation banned the production, sale, and transportation of alcoholic beverages, but the desire for alcohol persisted, leading to a thriving black market where criminals found another revenue stream.

In 1920, Luciano had already become acquainted with numerous future Mafia leaders, such as Vito Genovese and Frank Costello, with whom he maintained a long-lasting friendship and eventually became business partners through the Five Points Gang. Additionally, in the same year, Joe Masseria, a gang boss in Lower Manhattan, recruited Luciano as one of his gunmen. Around that time, Luciano and his close associates began collaborating with Arnold "The Brain" Rothstein, a gambler who recognized the potential profit to be made from Prohibition and taught Luciano about the logistics of running a bootlegging enterprise. With financial backing from Rothstein, Luciano, Costello, and Genovese established their own bootlegging operation.

Luciano received guidance from Rothstein in a variety of areas, including how to navigate high society. However, in 1923, Luciano's reputation suffered after he was caught selling heroin to undercover agents in a sting operation. While he didn't serve any prison time, the revelation that he was involved in drug trafficking caused harm to his reputation with his affluent peers and clients. To rehabilitate his image, Luciano purchased 200 high-priced seats to the Jack Dempsey-Luis Firpo boxing match in the Bronx, which he then distributed to top-level gangsters and politicians. Additionally, Rothstein accompanied Luciano on a shopping excursion to Wanamaker's Department Store in Manhattan to purchase costly clothing for the event. Their efforts were successful, and Luciano's reputation was ultimately restored.

In 1925, Luciano's illegal gambling and bootlegging ventures in New York, which also extended into Philadelphia, generated gross revenue of over $12 million annually. Additionally, Luciano's personal income amounted to roughly $4 million per year.

THE LATE 1920S

Luciano quickly rose to a prominent position in Joe Masseria's criminal enterprise. In contrast to Rothstein, Masseria lacked formal education, possessed poor manners, and had limited managerial abilities. By the late 1920s, Masseria's primary adversary was Salvatore Maranzano, who had arrived from Sicily to lead the Castellammarese clan. When one of Masseria's top lieutenants, Gaetano Reina, defected to Maranzano's side, Masseria instructed Luciano to orchestrate Reina's assassination. After Reina was killed on February 26, 1930, the feud between Masseria and Maranzano intensified, culminating in the brutal Castellammarese War.

CASTELLAMMARE SE WAR

The Castellammarese War was a violent struggle for supremacy within the Italian-American Mafia that took place in New York City from February 1930 to April 15, 1931. The conflict pitted supporters of Joe "The Boss" Masseria against those of Salvatore Maranzano and was named after Maranzano's birthplace of Castellammare del Golfo, Sicily. Maranzano's faction ultimately emerged victorious and divided New York's criminal organizations into the Five Families, with Maranzano declaring himself "boss of all bosses." However, Luciano ordered Maranzano's assassination in September 1931 and established the Commission, a power-sharing arrangement among Mafia families of equal status, to prevent future conflicts.

History

During the 1920s, the Mafia's activities in the United States were under the dominion of Giuseppe "Joe The Boss" Masseria, whose group consisted mostly of gangsters from Sicily, as well as from the southern Italian regions of Calabria (the 'Ndrangheta) and Campania (the Camorra). Members of Masseria's faction included Charles "Lucky" Luciano, Albert "Mad Hatter" Anastasia, Vito Genovese, Alfred Mineo, Willie Moretti, Joe Adonis, and Frank Costello. However, powerful Sicilian Don Vito Ferro aimed to take over control of the Mafia's operations, leading him to dispatch Salvatore Maranzano from his stronghold in Castellammare del Golfo to seize power. The Castellammarese group in the U.S. was made up of Joseph "Joe Bananas" Bonanno, Joseph Profaci, Joe Aiello, and Stefano "The Undertaker" Magaddino. As it became increasingly apparent that the two factions were headed for a clash over leadership of the Mafia, they endeavored to recruit more supporters to bolster their ranks.

On the surface, the Castellammarese War appeared to be a conflict between the supporters of Masseria and Maranzano. However, beneath the surface, there was also a generational divide between the old guard Sicilian leaders, known as the "Mustache Petes," who clung to traditional ways such as refusing to conduct business with non-Italians, and the "Young

Turks," a more diverse and forward-thinking group of Italian-Americans who had grown up in the U.S. Unlike the "Mustache Petes," the "Young Turks" were willing to work with non-Italians and were viewed as better suited to navigate the world of the 1930s. This approach led some of Masseria's followers to question his ability to lead the Mafia to prosperity. Led by Luciano, the "Young Turks" sought to end the war quickly so they could resume their businesses and modernize the Mafia by eliminating unnecessary traditions. Luciano's vision attracted followers who had grown disillusioned with Masseria's traditionalist leadership. As a result, both factions were fluid, with many mobsters switching sides or turning on their own allies during the war. Tensions between the Maranzano and Masseria factions had been building since as early as 1928, with both sides frequently hijacking each other's alcohol trucks, as the production of alcohol was illegal in the U.S. due to Prohibition at that time.

As the Castellammarese War escalated, armed gunmen clashed on the streets of New York City. According to Bonanno, in February 1930, Masseria ordered the assassination of Gaspar Milazzo, the president of Detroit's chapter of Unione Siciliana and a native of Castellammarese. Masseria was reportedly angered by Milazzo's refusal to support him in a dispute involving Al Capone and the Chicago Outfit.

The initial shot in the war was fired within

the Masseria faction when, on February 26, 1930, Masseria ordered the killing of a trusted ally, Gaetano Reina. Masseria assigned the job to a young Genovese, who used a shotgun to murder Reina. Masseria's objective was to protect his secret allies Tommy Lucchese, Dominick "The Gap" Petrilli, and finally Tommy Gagliano. However, Masseria's treachery would eventually come back to haunt him, as the Reina family later threw their support behind Maranzano. Additionally, Castellammarese-born members of Nicolo Schiro's gang began to pose a threat to Masseria's control over the Mafia gangs, with Vito Bonventre becoming a target. Masseria compelled Schiro to pay him $10,000 (equivalent to approximately $170,000 in 2022) and step down as the gang's boss. On July 15, 1930, Bonventre was fatally shot outside of his garage.

On August 15, 1930, supporters of the Castellammarese faction executed Giuseppe Morello, a key enforcer for Masseria, at Morello's East Harlem office. During the attack, Giuseppe Peraino, a visitor, was also killed. Two weeks later, Masseria suffered another setback when Joseph Pinzolo, whom he had appointed to oversee the ice-distribution racket after Reina's murder, was shot and killed on September 9 at a Times Square office rented by Lucchese, by members of the Reina family. Following these two killings, the Reina group officially joined forces with the Castellammarese.

However, Masseria didn't take these losses lying

down. On October 23, 1930, he struck back by ordering the assassination of Joe Aiello, a Chicago Unione Siciliane president and ally of the Castellammarese, in Chicago.

After the assassination of Aiello, the fortunes of the Castellammarese rapidly improved. On November 5, 1930, Mineo and Steve Ferrigno, a member of Masseria's gang, were murdered. Francesco Scalice took control of Mineo's gang and switched his allegiance to the Maranzano faction. Following Scalice's lead, many other members of Masseria's gang also began defecting to Maranzano, making the original battle lines of the conflict (Castellammarese versus non-Castellammarese) meaningless. On February 3, 1931, Joseph Catania, another important lieutenant of Masseria, was gunned down and died two days later.

As the situation worsened, Masseria's allies Luciano and Genovese began negotiating with Castellammarese leader Maranzano. They all agreed to betray Masseria if Maranzano would then end the war. A deal was reached, in which Luciano would arrange for Masseria's assassination and Maranzano would bring the Castellammarese War to a close. On April 15, 1931, in Nuova Villa Tammaro, a restaurant in Coney Island, Brooklyn Masseria was killed. While playing cards, Luciano purportedly excused himself to the bathroom, while Anastasia, Genovese, Joe Adonis, and Benjamin "Bugsy" Siegel allegedly carried out the assassination. Ciro "The

Artichoke King" Terranova drove the getaway car, but according to legend, he was too shaken up to drive and had to be pushed out of the driver's seat by Siegel.

However, according to The New York Times, "After that, the police have been unable to learn definitely [what happened]". Allegedly, Masseria was "seated at a table playing cards with two or three unknown men" when he was shot from behind. He died instantly from gunshot wounds to his head, chest, and back. Masseria's autopsy report revealed that he died on an empty stomach. No witnesses came forward, although "two or three" men were seen leaving the restaurant and getting into a stolen car. No one was convicted of Masseria's murder due to the lack of witnesses, and Luciano had an alibi.

Following Masseria's death, the Castellammarese War came to an end. Maranzano reorganized the Mafia in New York City, establishing a clear structure and hierarchy by dividing the major Italian gangs in the city into five families. Each family had a boss, underboss, consigliere, capos, soldiers, and associates. Although associates could come from any background, the higher ranks were required to be "made men," typically full-blooded Italian Americans. Shortly after the assassination, Maranzano announced that the Five Families would be led by Joe Bonanno, Joseph Profaci, Vincent Mangano, Thomas Gagliano, and Luciano.

Maranzano organized the major urban areas in the

Northeast and Midwest into one family per city, except for New York City, which was divided into five separate families due to the size of organized crime there. The bosses of the Five Families of New York were Luciano (now the Genovese crime family), Profaci (now the Colombo crime family), Gagliano (now the Lucchese crime family), Maranzano (now the Bonanno crime family), and finally Frank Scalice (now the Gambino crime family). Maranzano held a meeting of crime bosses in Wappingers Falls, New York, where he declared himself capo di tutti capi ("boss of all bosses").

Each crime family was led by a boss who was supported by an underboss. Later on, a consigliere was added to the hierarchy as the third-ranking position. Below the underboss, the family was divided into crews, each headed by a caporegime or capo and staffed by soldiers. Soldiers were often aided by associates, who were not yet members but worked closely with the family. Associates could include non-Italians who worked with the family, such as Meyer Lansky and Benjamin "Bugsy" Siegel.

THE END OF MARANZANO

Maranzano's time as capo di tutti capi was brief. While Maranzano was viewed as slightly more progressive than Masseria, Luciano believed he was even more rigid and power-hungry than his predecessor. On September 10, 1931, Maranzano was assassinated in his Manhattan office by a team of Jewish hitmen recruited by Lansky. The team included Samuel "Red" Levine, Bo Weinberg, and Bugsy Siegel, who shot and stabbed Maranzano to death.

After Maranzano and Masseria were eliminated, the Young Turks, led by Luciano, took control of the American Mafia in New York City. Their first priority was to restructure and reform the organization, and Luciano envisioned it as a major corporation, believing that this would reduce conflict, increase cooperation, and ensure efficient governance. Since

Maranzano had already created a basic structure, Luciano retained it, but with more flexibility to allow for the inclusion of other societal groups such as Jews. Bonanno's autobiography, A Man of Honor, describes the new system as one of leadership by committee, replacing the old custom of looking to one supreme leader for advice and dispute resolution. The most important men in the organization would assume the role of a parliamentary arrangement, formerly performed by one man.

After Maranzano's assassination, there were rumors of a massive purge of "old-timer" mafiosi, called the "Night of the Sicilian Vespers". Although this was seemingly confirmed by Joseph Valachi's testimony, a later study found no signs of such widespread violence. Luciano capitalized on the power vacuum to form "The Commission," an overseeing body for all Mafia activities in the US, tasked with mediating conflicts between families and eliminating the capo di tutti capi position.

Ultimately, the younger and more ruthless generation of mobsters, led by Luciano, emerged as the real victors of the war. With their ascent to power, organized crime was poised to expand into a national and multi-ethnic enterprise.

REORGANIZING LA COSA NOSTRA AND FORMING THE COMMISSION

Following the death of Maranzano, Luciano emerged as the most powerful crime boss in the United States. He rose to the top of the criminal underworld, setting policies and directing activities in coordination with other Mafia bosses. Under his leadership, his own crime family dominated lucrative criminal enterprises in New York City, including illegal gambling, extortion, bookmaking, loansharking, and drug trafficking. In addition, Luciano wielded significant influence in labor union activities and controlled a wide range of industries, including the Manhattan Waterfront, garbage hauling, construction, Garment District businesses, and trucking.

Luciano's leadership style differed from the previous bosses in that he preferred to operate behind the scenes and avoid drawing attention to himself. He saw the capo di tutti capi position as a source of conflict and instead maintained control by forming alliances with other bosses through the Commission. While he disagreed with Maranzano's traditional "made man" ceremony, he ultimately decided to keep it to promote obedience to the family. However, he remained committed to the oath of silence, or omertà, which served to protect the families from legal repercussions. Luciano also kept Maranzano's structure of five crime families in New York City, recognizing the benefits of this organizational framework.

Luciano placed his most loyal Italian associates in key positions within the Luciano crime family. Genovese became underboss and Costello served as consigliere. Caporegimes included Adonis, Michael "Trigger Mike" Coppola, Anthony Strollo, Willie Moretti, and Anthony Carfano. Since Lansky and Siegel were not Italian, they were not allowed to hold official positions in any Mafia family. However, Lansky was a trusted advisor to Luciano, and Siegel was a respected associate.

In 1931, Luciano proposed the creation of a Commission to govern organized crime during a meeting with various bosses in Chicago. The Commission would settle disputes and determine which families controlled which territories and was seen as Luciano's greatest innovation. His goal with the Commission was to maintain his own power over all the families while preventing future gang wars. The bosses approved the idea, and the Commission was established.

The Commission, consisting of representatives from the Five Families of New York City, the Buffalo crime family, and the Chicago Outfit, was established by Luciano in 1931 to govern organized crime in the United States. Later, the crime families of Philadelphia and Detroit were added to the Commission, with smaller families being represented by a Commission family. Even Jewish criminal organizations in New York had representation in the Commission.

The Commission's first major test came in 1935 when it ordered Dutch Schultz to abandon his plans to assassinate Special Prosecutor Thomas E. Dewey. Luciano was of the view that killing Dewey would trigger a massive law enforcement crackdown and that prosecutors and law enforcement officials were not to be harmed under any circumstances. Despite the Commission's ruling, Schultz refused to give up his plan to kill Dewey and left the meeting infuriated. Schultz even asked Murder, Inc leader Albert Anastasia to stake out Dewey's apartment building on Fifth Avenue. After learning this, the Commission held a meeting to discuss the matter and eventually ordered Lepke Buchalter to eliminate

Schultz. As a result, Schultz was shot in a tavern in Newark, New Jersey, on October 23, 1935, and died the following day, before he could carry out his plan to kill Dewey.

PROSECUTION
AND JAIL

In the early 1930s, Luciano's crime family began taking control of small-scale prostitution operations in New York City. However, their activities were disrupted when U.S. Attorney Thomas E. Dewey was appointed as a special prosecutor to combat organized crime in the city. One of Dewey's assistants, Eunice Carter, investigated prostitution racketeering and discovered evidence connecting Luciano to the network. Using wiretaps and interviews with prostitutes, Carter built a case and on February 2, 1936, Dewey authorized a raid on 200 brothels in Manhattan and Brooklyn. Carter took measures to prevent police corruption and trusted arrested prostitutes and madams to testify against the Mafia. By mid-March, several defendants had implicated Luciano as the ringleader of the prostitution ring.

Three of the prostitutes claimed that Luciano made collections, but the money actually went to Luciano's associate David Betillo.

In early 1936, Luciano was tipped off about an upcoming arrest and fled to Hot Springs, Arkansas. While there, a New York detective spotted him and alerted Dewey. On April 3, Luciano was arrested in Hot Springs on a criminal warrant from New York. The next day, he and his accomplices were indicted on 60 counts of compulsory prostitution. Luciano's lawyers in Arkansas fought hard against extradition, but after all their options were exhausted, Arkansas authorities handed him over to three New York City Police Department detectives on April 17 for transport back to New York. During the train transfer in St. Louis, they were guarded by 20 local policemen to prevent a rescue attempt. Luciano arrived in New York on April 18 and was sent to jail without bail. Meanwhile, Owney Madden, a former owner of the Cotton Club, attempted to bribe Arkansas Attorney General Carl E. Bailey with $50,000 to help Luciano's case, but Bailey refused and reported the bribe immediately.

Luciano's trial for pandering began on May 13, 1936, with Dewey prosecuting the case that Carter had built against him. Dewey accused Luciano of being part of a huge prostitution ring called "the Combination". Throughout the trial, Dewey relentlessly cross-examined Luciano and exposed him for lying on the witness stand, as well as for his relationships with well-known gangsters like Masseria, Terranova, and Buchalter.

Despite evidence that Luciano had profited from prostitution and members of his family ran a protection racket that ensnared many of New York City's madams and brothel keepers, some Mafia and legal scholars have questioned whether Luciano was directly involved in "the Combination". They believed that it would have been "out of character" for a crime boss of Luciano's stature to be directly involved in a prostitution ring.

Although the evidence Dewey presented against Luciano was considered "astonishingly thin" by some, on June 7, 1936, Luciano was convicted on 62 counts of compulsory prostitution. He was sentenced to 30 to 50 years in state prison, along with Betillo and others. Raab argued that it would have been more appropriate to charge Luciano with extortion and that Luciano's defense team made a mistake by allowing him to take the stand in his own defense, which opened the door for Dewey to attack his credibility on cross-examination.

According to some sources, Luciano's involvement in "the Combination" has been contested, including by his contemporaries Polly Adler and Joe Bonanno. Adler, a New York madam, claimed that if Luciano had been involved, she would have known about it, while Bonanno suggested that Luciano's name was used by some of his soldiers to intimidate brothel owners into paying for protection. However, several key witnesses at Luciano's trial testified that he was heavily involved in prostitution racketeering, discussing the industry frequently and comparing it to chain stores. Luciano also reportedly hired individuals to collect kickbacks from bookers and madams, operating from his Waldorf-Astoria suite. Despite debates about the extent of his involvement, Luciano was convicted on 62 counts of compulsory prostitution and sentenced to 30-50 years in prison.

From behind bars, Luciano maintained control over his crime family, communicating his orders through acting boss Genovese. However, when Genovese fled to Naples in 1937 to avoid an imminent murder indictment, Luciano appointed his consigliere, Costello, as the new acting boss and overseer of his interests.

Initially imprisoned at Sing Sing Correctional Facility, Luciano was later transferred to Clinton Correctional Facility, a remote facility far from New York City. There, Betillo, one of Luciano's associates, prepared special dishes for him in a kitchen set aside by authorities. Despite being assigned to work in the prison laundry, Luciano used his influence to have a church built at the prison, which became known for its freestanding structure and the inclusion of two original doors from Ferdinand Magellan's ship on the altar.

Luciano's legal appeals dragged on until October 10, 1938, when the U.S. Supreme Court declined to review his case. At this point, Luciano resigned as the head of his crime family, and Costello officially took over his position.

WORLD
WAR 2 AND
DEPORTATION

During World War II, the US government made a confidential agreement with Luciano, who was still in prison. In 1942, the Office of Naval Intelligence was concerned about the possibility of German and Italian agents entering the US through the New York waterfront, as well as the possibility of sabotage in these facilities. The US Navy decided to contact Lansky to negotiate a deal with Luciano, as they knew that the Mafia controlled the waterfront. To facilitate negotiations, Luciano was transferred to Great Meadow Correctional Facility in Comstock, New York, which was much closer to New York City.

After some negotiations, the Navy, the State of New York, and Luciano reached an agreement: Luciano would receive a commutation of his sentence in exchange for his organization's full cooperation in providing intelligence to the Navy. Anastasia, who was an ally of Luciano and controlled the docks, allegedly promised that there would be no dockworker strikes during the war. As the 1943 allied invasion of Sicily approached, it is believed that Luciano provided the US military with contacts within the Sicilian Mafia.. This collaboration between the Mafia and the US Navy became known as Operation Underworld.

The value of Luciano's contribution to the war effort is disputed, with different reports giving different assessments. In 1947, the naval officer who oversaw Operation Underworld downplayed the significance of Luciano's contribution to the war effort. However, a 1954 report commissioned by Governor Dewey concluded that Luciano had provided numerous valuable services to Naval Intelligence. Luciano alleged that the enemy threat to the docks was manufactured by the sinking of the SS Normandie in New York harbor, but the official investigation found no evidence of sabotage.

As a presumed reward for his alleged wartime cooperation, Dewey commuted Luciano's sentence on the condition that he not resist deportation to Italy. Luciano accepted the deal and was transported to Ellis Island for deportation proceedings. On February 10, Luciano's ship sailed from Brooklyn Harbor for Italy, and on arrival, he told reporters he would likely reside in Sicily.

MOVING TO HAVANA, CUBA

In October 1946, Luciano moved to Havana, Cuba, using a complex route to conceal his travels. He took a freighter from Naples to Caracas, Venezuela, then flew to Rio de Janeiro, Brazil, before heading to Mexico City and returning to Caracas. From there, he flew to Camagüey, Cuba, and finally arrived in Havana on October 29. He settled into an estate in the Miramar neighborhood, with the goal of being closer to the US and eventually regaining control over American Mafia operations.

Lansky was already involved in Cuban gambling and hotel projects and arranged a meeting of the major crime families at the Hotel Nacional de Cuba in December 1946. The gathering, known as the Havana Conference, was ostensibly for the purpose of seeing Frank Sinatra perform, but the real agenda was to discuss important mob business. Luciano attended the conference, which lasted over a week and covered topics such as the heroin trade, Cuban gambling, and how to address issues with Siegel's Flamingo Hotel project in Las Vegas.

During the Havana Conference on December 20, Luciano held a private meeting with Genovese in his hotel suite. Genovese had recently returned from Italy to New York, where his 1934 murder charge had been dismissed, allowing him to resume his role in the mob. Luciano had never fully trusted Genovese, and during the meeting, Genovese proposed that Luciano become a "boss of bosses" in name only and allow him to run everything behind the scenes. Luciano calmly declined Genovese's suggestion.

After the Havana Conference had begun, the US government became aware of Luciano's presence in Cuba. Luciano had been publicly socializing with Sinatra and visiting many nightclubs, making his location no secret in Havana. The US government started to pressure the Cuban government to expel him.

On February 21, 1947, U.S. Narcotics Commissioner Harry J. Anslinger informed the Cubans that the US would block all shipments of narcotic prescription drugs while Luciano remained there. Just 48 hours later, the Cuban government declared that Lucky Luciano was in custody and would be deported to Italy within two days. Luciano was subsequently placed on a freighter that was sailing to Genoa.

BACK TO ITALY

Following Luciano's deportation to Italy, he was under strict police surveillance for the rest of his life. Upon his arrival in Genoa on April 11, 1947, he was arrested and taken to a jail in Palermo. However, on May 11, he was released with a warning to stay out of trouble.

In July 1949, Luciano was arrested in Rome on suspicion of being involved in the shipment of narcotics to New York. He was released a week later without charges but was permanently banned from visiting Rome. In 1951, he was questioned by police in Naples for allegedly illegally bringing cash and a new car into Italy, but was released without any charges after 20 hours of questioning.

In 1952, the Italian government revoked Luciano's passport due to complaints from US and Canadian law enforcement officials. On November 1, 1954, an Italian judicial commission in Naples imposed strict limitations on Luciano, requiring him to report to the police every Sunday, stay home every night, and not leave Naples without police permission for a period of two years. The commission cited his alleged involvement in the narcotics trade as the reason for these restrictions.

In 1957, Genovese, with the help of the Anastasia family underboss Carlo Gambino, decided to make a move against Luciano and his acting boss, Costello. On May 2 of that year, Vincent "Chin" Gigante carried out Genovese's orders by ambushing Costello in the lobby of his Central Park apartment building, The Majestic. Gigante shouted, "This is for you, Frank," and shot Costello in the head as he turned around. Gigante fled the scene, believing he had successfully killed Costello. However, the bullet only grazed Costello's head, and he sustained no serious injuries. Despite his reluctance to cooperate with law enforcement, Gigante was arrested for attempted murder. He was later acquitted at trial and thanked Costello in the courtroom after the verdict. Costello, who had lost control of the Genovese crime family to Genovese, was allowed to retire. Luciano was unable to prevent the power shift.

In 1957, Genovese and Gambino arranged the assassination of Anastasia, who was also an ally of Luciano. The next month, Genovese called a meeting of crime bosses in Apalachin, New York to gain approval for his takeover of the Luciano family and to assert his national power. However, the meeting went awry when law enforcement conducted a raid, resulting in over 65 high-ranking mobsters being arrested and the Mafia receiving negative publicity and grand jury summonses. Many of the angry mobsters blamed Genovese for the debacle, which created an opportunity for his opponents to strike back.

According to reports, Luciano was present at a gathering in a hotel in Palermo to discuss the heroin trade, which was part of the French Connection. Following the meeting in Palermo, Luciano allegedly helped pay a Puerto Rican drug dealer $100,000 to falsely implicate Genovese in a drug deal. Genovese was eventually found guilty of conspiracy to violate federal narcotics laws on April 4, 1959, and was sentenced to 15 years in prison. Despite being incarcerated, Genovese attempted to maintain control of his crime family until his death in 1969. As a result, Gambino emerged as the most influential figure in the Cosa Nostra.

DEATH

Luciano passed away on January 26, 1962, due to a heart attack at Naples International Airport. He had gone there to meet with American producer Martin Gosch regarding a film based on his life. Luciano had previously refused to authorize a film to avoid antagonizing other Mafia members, but reportedly relented after the death of his longtime lover, Igea Lissoni. Unfortunately, Luciano was unaware that Italian drug agents had followed him to the airport in anticipation of arresting him on drug smuggling charges.

Luciano's funeral service was held in Naples three days later and was attended by 300 people. His body was taken through the streets of Naples in a horse-drawn black hearse. With permission from the US government, Luciano's relatives transported his body back to New York to be buried. He was laid to rest in St. John's Cemetery in Middle Village, Queens, and over 2,000 mourners attended his funeral. Gambino, Luciano's longtime friend, gave the eulogy. In 1998, Time magazine referred to Luciano as the "criminal mastermind" among the top 20 most influential builders and titans of the 20th century.

THE LEGACY OF LUCKY LUCIANO: THE MAN AND THE MYTH

In conclusion, Charles "Lucky" Luciano was a notorious American mobster who rose to fame in the early 20th century. He was a key figure in the development of modern organized crime, and his influence is still felt today in the world of organized crime. This chapter will examine the legacy of Lucky Luciano, both the man and the myth, and how he has influenced organized crime to this day.

Luciano was born Salvatore Lucania in Sicily, Italy in 1897. He moved to New York with his family in 1906 and quickly became involved in street gangs and other criminal activities. By the age of 18, he was a member of the Five Points Gang, one of the most powerful criminal organizations in New York at the time. Luciano was known for his intelligence, strategic thinking, and ability to stay out of the spotlight.

In the 1920s, Luciano played a key role in the formation of the National Crime Syndicate, which brought together various criminal organizations across the United States. Luciano helped to create a more organized and efficient criminal underworld, which led to increased profits and power for organized crime bosses.

In 1931, Luciano was instrumental in the formation of the Commission, which was a governing body made up of the bosses of the major crime families in New York City. The Commission established a code of conduct for organized crime, which included rules about how to divide territory, how to settle disputes, and how to deal with law enforcement. The Commission also helped to solidify Luciano's position as one of the most powerful and influential mobsters in the United States.

During World War II, Luciano allegedly helped the US Navy by providing intelligence about the Sicilian Mafia. After the war, Luciano became involved in the heroin trade, which was known as the French Connection. He allegedly used his connections to the Sicilian Mafia to smuggle heroin into the United States, and his involvement in the drug trade helped to solidify the power of organized crime in America.

Despite his criminal activities, Luciano has been the subject of numerous books, movies, and television shows. He is often portrayed as a charismatic and intelligent figure who was able to bring together warring factions of organized crime. However, his true legacy is more complicated. While he was certainly a shrewd businessman and a key figure in the development of organized crime, he was also a ruthless and violent criminal who was responsible for numerous murders and other illegal activities.

Charles "Lucky" Luciano was a complex and influential figure in the history of organized crime. His legacy can be seen in the continued influence of the National Crime Syndicate and the Commission, as well as in the continued presence of organized crime in American society. Despite his criminal activities, Luciano remains a fascinating and controversial figure, and his legacy continues to be debated and discussed today.

MEYER LANSKY

THE LIFE AND TIMES OF MEYER LANSKY

Meyer Lansky was one of the most enigmatic and influential figures of the 20th century American organized crime. He was a key member of the notorious mafia syndicate known as the "The Syndicate" and a trusted adviser to some of the most powerful underworld bosses of his time. Lansky was known as a mastermind of gambling operations, illegal money-laundering schemes, and international crime syndicates that spanned across the globe. Despite his reputation as a ruthless and cunning mobster, Lansky was also a visionary businessman who transformed the gambling industry and invested heavily in legitimate businesses.

Born in 1902 to Jewish immigrants in Poland,

Lansky moved to New York City at a young age and quickly became involved in organized crime. He rose through the ranks of the Jewish mob in the 1920s and 1930s, working alongside some of the most notorious gangsters of his time, including Lucky Luciano, Bugsy Siegel, and Frank Costello. Together, they created a vast criminal empire that controlled gambling, prostitution, and racketeering throughout the United States.

Throughout his career, Lansky remained largely elusive and mysterious, often avoiding the spotlight and keeping a low profile. He rarely spoke to the media, preferring to operate behind the scenes and maintain his influence through careful negotiations and strategic alliances. Lansky was also known for his diplomatic skills, often mediating disputes between rival factions and keeping the peace among warring gangs.

Despite his notoriety, Lansky remained an enigmatic and complex figure, with conflicting accounts of his life and legacy. Some viewed him as a criminal mastermind, while others saw him as a savvy businessman and investor. Regardless of one's perspective, Lansky's life and career offer a unique and fascinating glimpse into the world of organized crime and the complex networks of power, money, and influence that shaped American society in the 20th century. This book aims to provide a comprehensive and engaging portrait of Meyer Lansky, exploring his life, his influence, and his enduring legacy.

EARLY LIFE

Born as Maier Suchowljansky on July 4, 1902, in Grodno (now Belarus), Meyer Lansky's early years were marked by poverty, persecution, and a turbulent political climate in the Russian Empire. Along with his family, he faced discrimination and violence from the Imperial authorities due to their Polish-Jewish heritage. In 1911, Lansky arrived in the United States with his mother and brother Jacob, and joined his father, who had already settled on the Lower East Side of Manhattan. It was there that he would meet two individuals who would shape the course of his life: Benjamin "Bugsy" Siegel and Charles "Lucky" Luciano.

Siegel and Lansky, childhood friends turned partners, were involved in the bootlegging trade during Prohibition, running one of the most notorious and violent gangs of the era, the Bugs and Meyer Mob. Lansky's relationship with Luciano was different; they initially met when Luciano attempted to extort him for protection money, but instead, the two formed an unlikely bond. Luciano recognized Lansky's defiance and intelligence and proposed a partnership that would extend beyond their teenage years. Their association with veteran gangster Arnold Rothstein brought them further into the criminal underworld.

By 1929, Luciano had a grand vision for a national crime syndicate that would unite the Italian, Jewish, and Irish gangs and transform organized crime into a profitable business. Along with Lansky, Johnny Torrio, and Frank Costello, they held a conference in Atlantic City, which marked the birth of the syndicate.

GAMBLING
OPERATIONS

I n 1936, Maier Suchowljansky, better known as Meyer Lansky, had already made a name for himself in the criminal underworld. He had successfully established gambling operations in Florida, New Orleans, and Cuba, which were considered innovative for their time. Lansky's success can be attributed to two key factors. Firstly, he had a deep understanding of the mathematical odds of popular wagering games, which allowed him to manage his operations with great efficiency. Secondly, Lansky relied on his extensive mob connections and bribery of law enforcement officials to ensure the legal and physical security of his establishments, protecting them from both rival crime figures and law enforcement agencies. These two innovations helped Lansky become a prominent figure in the world of organized crime, and solidified his reputation as a skilled and successful operator.

Lansky's reputation for integrity extended beyond the fairness of his gambling operations. Unlike other "clip joints" that rigged games and cheated customers, Lansky's "carpet joints" maintained a strict rule of integrity. He made sure that the staff responsible for administering the games were men of high moral character.

As his empire expanded, Lansky recognized the importance of protecting himself from prosecution. In 1946, he persuaded the Italian-American Mafia to install Siegel as the head of the Flamingo Hotel in Las Vegas, in which Lansky became a major investor. To evade potential prosecution for tax evasion and prostitution, Lansky channeled the illegal earnings from his casino businesses into a Swiss bank account that provided anonymity under the 1934 Swiss Banking Act. Subsequently, he purchased an offshore bank in Switzerland, through which he laundered money using a network of shell and holding companies.

WORLD WAR 2

During the 1930s, Maier Lansky and his gang members extended their activities beyond their typical criminal endeavors to combat the pro-Nazi German-American Bund. In particular, Lansky recalled an incident in which he and fourteen of his associates disrupted a rally in Yorkville, a German neighborhood in Manhattan. The stage was adorned with a swastika and an image of Adolf Hitler, and the speakers launched into a tirade. Despite being vastly outnumbered, Lansky and his group took action, throwing some of the Nazis out of the windows and chasing and assaulting others who attempted to flee. Their aim was to demonstrate that Jews would not sit back and tolerate such insults.

OPERATION UNDERWORLD

Operation Underworld was a collaborative effort between the United States government and Italian and Jewish organized crime figures from 1942 to 1945. The operation aimed to counter Axis spies and saboteurs along the northeastern seaboard ports, prevent wartime labor union strikes, and limit theft of vital war supplies and equipment by black-marketeers. The Mafia boss Albert Anastasia's claim of responsibility for the alleged sabotage and sinking of the Normandie (renamed Lafayette for war service) in February 1942 led to suspicion of Mafia sabotage. While the United States government claimed the loss of the Normandie was an accident, many Americans remained skeptical and believed that the destruction was planned by the Nazis. Several Axis spies and saboteurs were arrested and executed during the operation, but no evidence was produced to link Axis spies to the loss of the Normandie.

Commander Charles R. Haffenden of the U.S. Navy Office of Naval Intelligence (ONI) Third Naval District in New York had concerns about the potential for sabotage or disruption of the waterfront during World War II. To address this, he established a special security unit and enlisted the help of Joseph Lanza, who oversaw the Fulton Fish Market, to gather intelligence about the New York waterfront, manage labor unions, and locate potential refueling and resupply operations for German submarines with the assistance of the fishing industry along the Atlantic Coast.

To conceal Lanza's activities, Haffenden reached out to Meyer Lansky for assistance in contacting Charles Luciano, a powerful boss of the five New York Mafia crime families. Luciano agreed to cooperate with authorities in hopes of receiving early release from prison.

In 1936, Charles "Lucky" Luciano was convicted of running a prostitution racket and sentenced to 30 to 50 years in prison after a lengthy investigation by District Attorney Thomas E. Dewey. However, during World War II, an agreement was struck between Luciano's associate Meyer Lansky and the Department of the Navy, in which Luciano would provide naval intelligence in exchange for a commuted sentence. As a result, in 1946, Luciano's sentence was commuted on the condition that he be deported to Italy.

Luciano's contacts proved valuable to the Allies during the 1943 amphibious invasion of Sicily, providing maps of the island's harbors, photographs of its coastline, and trusted contacts within the Sicilian Mafia who also wished to see Mussolini toppled. Luciano even directed Calogero Vizzini to assist the Allied Forces in the invasion, who spent six days on an American tank, guiding Allied forces through the mountain pass and directing his Sicilian Mafia to take out Italian snipers in the mountains.

At the time of Operation Underworld, Charles "Lucky" Luciano was serving a 30 to 50-year sentence in Dannemora for running a prostitution ring. However, his sentence was commuted in 1946 and he was deported to Italy, due in part to his cooperation with the authorities during World War II. While it is unclear whether Luciano's influence played a significant role in stopping sabotage, it is noted that strikes on the docks ceased after his attorney Moses Polakoff contacted underworld figures with influence over the longshoremen and their unions. In May 1942, Luciano was moved to a more convenient and comfortable open prison in Great Meadows.

CUBA AND THE FLAMINGO HOTEL

In 1946, Meyer Lansky attended a secretive meeting in Havana to discuss the mismanagement of the Flamingo Hotel by his friend and partner, Benjamin "Bugsy" Siegel. The Mafia investors were losing a lot of money due to the project's delays and cost overruns. Despite the others wanting to kill Siegel, Lansky pleaded with them to give his friend another chance. Siegel's fortunes did turn around temporarily, but the Flamingo ultimately continued to lose money. Another meeting was called, and this time, Lansky and Luciano convinced the other investors to give Siegel more time. However, when the hotel continued to struggle financially, the other investors decided that Siegel was finished. There is speculation that Lansky may have been involved in the decision to eliminate Siegel, given his stature in the organization and his long relationship with Siegel. On June 20, 1947, Siegel was shot and killed in Beverly Hills, California.

Following Siegel's death, Lansky's associates assumed control of the Flamingo hotel. Lansky reportedly maintained a significant financial interest in the hotel for the next two decades, according to the FBI. Although his role was less prominent than before, Lansky is believed to have advised and helped Chicago boss Tony Accardo establish his dominance in Vegas, marking a power transfer from New York's Five Families to the Chicago Outfit. Despite his involvement, Lansky later claimed in interviews that he would have preferred that Siegel had remained alive.

As a reward for his wartime service, Luciano's sentence for pandering was commuted to time served after World War II. However, he was forced to accept deportation to his native Italy and give up his American citizenship. Upon arrival, Luciano settled in Sicily but eventually moved to Cuba to resume control over Mafia operations. While there, he ran several casinos with the blessing of Cuban dictator Fulgencio Batista. Their relationship led to a lucrative business deal that lasted a decade. Lansky and Batista agreed that, in exchange for kickbacks, the Mafia would gain control of the country's casinos and racetracks. With Batista's help, Lansky would centralize Cuba's gambling operations, and the government would match any hotel investment over $1 million and grant a casino license. To kick off the plan, Lansky called for a summit of his associates in Havana.

On December 22, 1946, the Havana Conference took place at the Hotel Nacional. This was a significant gathering of American underworld leaders, and the first of its kind since the Chicago meeting in 1932. Attendees included notorious figures such as Albert "The Mad Hatter" Anastasia, Vito Genovese, Frank Costello, and Joseph "Joe Bananas" Bonanno. Also present were representatives of the Jewish interest, including Lansky, Moe Dalitz, and "Dandy" Phil Kastel from Florida.

Luciano, who arrived first with a false passport, was appointed as kingpin for the mob according to his account of the events. Lansky shared his vision of a new Havana, one that would be profitable for those willing to invest the right amount of money. Entertainment at the conference was provided by the likes of Frank Sinatra, who flew to Cuba with his friends, the Fischetti brothers. The conference was a pivotal moment in the history of organized crime and laid the groundwork for the Mafia's domination of the Cuban gambling industry.

In 1952, Lansky made a proposition to then-President Carlos Prío Socarrás, offering him a bribe of $250,000 to resign and make way for Batista's return to power. After Batista seized control of the government through a military coup in March of that year, gambling was quickly reinstated. Lansky was offered an unofficial role as the gambling minister with an annual salary of $25,000. By 1955, Batista had changed the gambling laws yet again, allowing anyone who invested $1 million in a hotel or $200,000 in a nightclub to receive a gaming license without undergoing background checks. Venture capitalists who made the required investment were granted tax exemptions, duty-free importation of equipment and furnishings, and public matching funds for construction. In exchange, the government received $250,000 for each license issued, as well as a share of the profits from each casino. Batista's brother-in-law, Roberto Fernandez y Miranda, was appointed to oversee the 10,000 slot machines in Cuba, while also being given ownership of the parking meters in Havana. Import duties were waived on materials for hotel construction, and insiders profited from importing surplus materials and selling them at inflated prices. It was rumored that politicians received periodic payoffs and sometimes required more than the $250,000 license fee under the table.

Lansky worked to revamp the Cabaret Montmartre and turn it into the hottest spot in Havana. Additionally, he oversaw the installation of a casino at the Hotel Nacional. Despite objections from other American expatriates, including Ernest Hemingway, Lansky gained support from Batista.

Once all the new hotels, nightclubs, and casinos were built, Batista wasted no time collecting his share of the profits. Every night, the "bagman" for Batista's wife Marta collected 10% of the profits from Trafficante's interests, including the Sans Souci cabaret and the casinos in the Sevilla-Biltmore, Commodoro, Deauville, and Capri hotels. Batista's take from Lansky's casinos, such as his prized Habana Riviera, the Nacional, and the Montmartre, among others, was said to be 30%. However, the exact amount that Batista and his associates received in the form of bribes, payoffs, and profiteering has never been confirmed. The regime's bank account was boosted by around $1 million from the revenue generated by slot machines alone..

Following the Cuban Revolution and Fidel Castro's rise to power in 1959, mob investment in Cuba became untenable. While Batista was preparing to flee to the Dominican Republic on New Year's Eve 1958, Lansky was celebrating the US$3 million profit he made in the first year of operations at the Habana Riviera, his US$8 million palace. However, many of the casinos, including several of Lansky's, were looted and destroyed that night.

Castro marched into Havana on January 8, 1959, and set up a command post in the Hilton, while Lansky fled the day before. The new Cuban president, Manuel Urrutia Lleó, took action to close the casinos, and in October 1960, Castro nationalized all of the island's hotel-casinos and banned gambling. This move wiped out Lansky's assets and revenue streams, resulting in an estimated loss of $7 million. With the crackdown on casinos in Miami, Lansky was forced to rely on his Las Vegas profits. As a result, he sought compensation from the U.S. government for his losses in Cuba.

IMMAGRATION TO ISREAL AND SUBSEQUENT TRIAL

I n 1970, Meyer Lansky fled to Israel to escape federal tax evasion charges in the United States. However, two years later, he was deported back to the U.S. to stand trial. Lansky's trial took place in 1974 with the testimony of loan shark Vincent "Fat Vinnie" Teresa. Despite the government's efforts to convict him, Lansky was acquitted.

BLACKMAIL OF J. EDGAR HOOVER

According to various sources, including biographer Anthony Summers' book Official and Confidential: The Secret Life of J. Edgar Hoover, Meyer Lansky is said to have had "controlled" sexually compromising photographs of former FBI director J. Edgar Hoover with his aide Clyde Tolson. Summers cites multiple primary sources regarding Lansky's use of blackmail to gain influence with politicians, law enforcement officials, and judges. One avenue for acquiring blackmail material was allegedly through orgies hosted by Lansky protégé Roy Cohn and liquor magnate Lewis Rosenstiel, who had ties with the Mafia from his bootlegging days during Prohibition. Despite extensive monitoring and investigation by the FBI, as revealed in released FBI files on Lansky, it is unclear why he was never convicted. Some speculate that he successfully evaded conviction by using blackmail, a model which was reportedly copied by Cohn himself to control politicians and evade conviction.

DEATH

Lansky settled into retirement in Miami, where he spent his final years at his home in Miami Beach, Florida. He passed away on January 15, 1983, at the age of 80, survived by his wife and three children. Despite his reputation as a financial wizard, Lansky's personal finances were in dire straits in his later years. His biographer, Robert Lacey, reported that Lansky struggled to pay for his handicapped son's healthcare, and the family was living in poverty.

Although the FBI believed that Lansky left behind hidden bank accounts worth over $300 million, no money was ever found. According to Lacey, there was no evidence to support the notion that Lansky was the mastermind behind organized crime in America. In fact, his wealth and influence had been greatly exaggerated, and he was far from the "king of all evil." At the time of his death, Lansky was worth almost nothing on paper. His second wife's granddaughter reported that he left behind only

$57,000 in cash.

Lansky himself admitted that he had "crapped out" in Cuba, where he claimed to have lost almost every penny. Despite his financial troubles, Lansky remained unrepentant and never made excuses for his actions.

Hank Messick, a journalist who investigated Lansky extensively, believed that the true source of Lansky's power was not in his property ownership but in the people around him whom he controlled. Messick once said, "Meyer Lansky doesn't own property. He owns people." While the FBI and Manhattan District Attorney Robert Morgenthau believed that Lansky had kept large sums of money in other people's names for years, Messick argued that this was nothing new for Lansky and that he had always kept very little in his own name.

In 2010, Lansky's daughter Sandra revealed that her father had transferred about $15 million to his brother's account in the early 1970s when he was having trouble with the IRS. However, it remains unclear how much money Lansky actually had at his disposal. Since the warming of relations between the US and Cuba in 2015, Lansky's grandson, Gary Rapoport, has been seeking compensation from the Cuban government for the seizure of the Riviera Hotel, which was built by his grandfather in Havana. The exact amount of wealth Lansky possessed is likely to remain a mystery.

LEGACY

In conclusion, Meyer Lansky was one of the most influential and enigmatic figures in American organized crime history. He was a mastermind of the gambling industry, and his political connections enabled him to become a powerful and wealthy figure in the world of organized crime. Lansky was a shrewd businessman who always stayed one step ahead of the law, which made him a key player in the underworld for decades.

While Lansky was often portrayed as a ruthless and greedy gangster, recent research and interviews with family members have suggested a more nuanced view of the man. His wealth and influence were often exaggerated, and he struggled with financial difficulties later in life. Nevertheless, there is no doubt that Lansky was an important figure in American organized crime, and his legacy continues to be felt to this day.

Despite his involvement in illegal activities, Lansky was also known for his philanthropic efforts, particularly in his later years. He made significant contributions to Jewish charities and causes and was involved in efforts to help Israel. In this way, Lansky's legacy is complicated, as he was both a criminal and a philanthropist.

Overall, Meyer Lansky's life and legacy continue to fascinate and intrigue scholars, historians, and the public alike. His role in American organized crime history is undeniable, and his influence on the gambling industry is still felt to this day. Despite the controversy and criminal activity associated with his name, there is no doubt that Meyer Lansky was a complex and fascinating figure in American history.

BENJAMIN
"BUGSY" SIEGEL

BUGSY

B ugsy Siegel was a notorious American mobster who rose to power in the mid-20th century, becoming one of the most infamous and influential figures of organized crime in the United States. He was a charismatic and ruthless leader who pursued wealth, power, and fame through his involvement in gambling, bootlegging, and other criminal enterprises. Siegel was also a complex and enigmatic figure, who defied easy categorization or explanation. Some saw him as a visionary entrepreneur who helped transform Las Vegas from a dusty desert town into a glittering gambling oasis, while others saw him as a violent thug who left a trail of blood and destruction in his wake.

This book tells the story of Bugsy Siegel, exploring his life, his crimes, and his legacy. Drawing on a wide range of sources, including court records, police reports, historical archives, and interviews with surviving associates and family members, the book provides a detailed and vivid portrait of Siegel, his associates, and his world. It explores his rise to power in the criminal underworld, his role in the development of Las Vegas, and his relationships with other mobsters, Hollywood celebrities, and political figures. It also delves into Siegel's personal life, including his love affairs, family relationships, and psychological profile.

The book presents a nuanced and comprehensive account of Siegel's life and times, challenging many of the myths and legends that have grown up around him. It shows how Siegel embodied both the promise and the peril of the American dream, and how his legacy continues to shape our understanding of crime, power, and the allure of the outlaw. Whether you are a fan of true crime, a student of American history, or simply a curious reader, this book offers a compelling and illuminating portrait of one of the most fascinating figures in modern American history.

BEGINNINGS AND THE BUGS AND MEYER MOB

Born on February 28, 1906, in the Williamsburg neighborhood of Brooklyn, Benjamin Siegel was the second of five children in a poor Ashkenazi Jewish family that emigrated to the U.S. from Austria-Hungary. His parents, Jennie and Max Siegel, worked constantly for low wages, and as a result, Siegel left school at a young age and fell in with a gang on the Lower East Side of Manhattan.

Siegel initially committed mainly thefts, but his criminal activities escalated when he met Moe Sedway. Together, they developed a protection racket in which they threatened to burn the merchandise of pushcart owners unless they paid a dollar. This marked the beginning of Siegel's career in organized crime.

As he grew older, Siegel's criminal record expanded to include armed robbery, rape, and murder. Despite this, he remained a charismatic figure and was admired by many for his style, wit, and charm.

THE MOB

L ansky and his associates formed a protective society to safeguard themselves against the Italian and Irish gangs. The group comprised of Lansky, his brother Jacob, Meyer "Mike" Wassell, Samuel "Red" Levine, Irving "Tabbo" Sandler, Joseph "Doc" Stacher, and others. However, there are conflicting accounts of how Lansky met Siegel. One version suggests that Lansky intervened in a dispute between Siegel and Charles Luciano over a prostitute, while another, according to Lansky's official biographies, claims they met on a street corner in Lower East Side Manhattan as teenagers. In the latter account, Lansky prevented Siegel from using a gun during a fight, causing the latter to become angry initially but ultimately leading to a close friendship between the two. Siegel was known for his physical strength and aggression, while Lansky was known for his intellect, earning them the nicknames "brawn" and "brains," respectively. Siegel's volatile personality earned him the moniker

"Bugsy," which he disliked.

In the early 1920s, Lansky and Siegel founded the Bugs and Meyer mob, which collaborated with Charles "Lucky" Luciano and his associate Frank Costello. The group recruited sharpshooters and facilitated bootleggers with stolen vehicles and drivers, with Lansky's expertise in mechanics and automobiles proving to be an asset. Abner "Longie" Zwillman, Irving Zwillman, Moe Sedway, and Louis "Lepke" Buchalter later joined the gang, which engaged in illegal activities like providing protection, truck hijacking, murder, and unlawful gambling. They also acted as enforcers for Costello, both in New York and Louisiana, and were instrumental in eliminating or subjugating most of the Italian-American gangs using tactics such as assassination and political bribery.

The Bugs and Meyer mob's violent notoriety grew as they extorted money from various groups, including Jewish moneylenders and storekeepers, as well as Italian and Irish shop owners and gamblers. The group concealed their illegal activities by operating a car and truck rental garage, which served as a warehouse for stolen goods. Lansky and Siegel, having close ties to Luciano, often employed the gang to collaborate with Joe Adonis's Broadway Mob throughout the 1920s. The New York City Police Department described the gang as "vicious," and a veteran detective recounted Siegel's pleasure in witnessing the suffering and death of his victims. During the Castellammarese War, Lansky and Siegel helped Luciano organize the modern American Mafia by eliminating the "Mustache Petes." Siegel was believed to be among the hitmen who killed Joe Masseria, and Lansky assisted Luciano in the murder of Salvatore Maranzano by enlisting Jewish hitmen. When Lansky and Luciano established the National Crime Syndicate in the 1930s, they advocated for an outfit specifically for "enforcement" or murders for the syndicate, which became known as Murder, Inc. Bugs and Meyer mob members served as advisers or hitmen for Murder, Inc. when it was later led by Lepke Buchalter and Albert Anastasia.

CALIFORNIA

Siegel became aware of a threat to his life as his hospital alibi became suspect, and his enemies wanted him dead. In the late 1930s, the East Coast mob sent Siegel to California, where he had previously visited several times since 1933, to establish syndicate-approved gambling operations with Los Angeles family boss Jack Dragna. Siegel recruited Mickey Cohen as his top lieutenant and, backed by Lansky and Luciano, convinced Dragna to accept a subordinate position. Siegel claimed legal gambling as his source of income on tax returns, but he soon took control of Los Angeles's numbers racket and facilitated a drug trade route from Mexico while establishing circuits with the Chicago Outfit's wire services.

By 1942, the syndicate's bookmaking wire operations were generating $500,000 per day. Despite complications with the wire services, Siegel managed several offshore casinos and a major prostitution ring, as well as maintained relationships with various individuals such as politicians, businessmen, attorneys, accountants, and lobbyists who acted as his front. However, Siegel's problems with the wire services eventually led to the Outfit taking over the Continental Press in 1946, giving the racing wire percentage to Dragna, which infuriated Siegel.

Siegel quickly gained acceptance in the upper echelons of Hollywood and formed close relationships with famous actors such as Clark Gable, Cary Grant, Gary Cooper, and George Raft, as well as studio executives including Louis B. Mayer and Jack L. Warner. He was even able to count actress Jean Harlow as a friend and godmother to his daughter Millicent. Siegel's lavish Beverly Hills home was the site of many extravagant parties that were attended by young celebrities like Tony Curtis, Phil Silvers, and Frank Sinatra.

In addition to his Hollywood connections, Siegel was also involved with several prominent women, including Countess Dorothy di Frasso, whom he traveled with to Italy in 1938. While there, he met with infamous leaders such as Benito Mussolini, Hermann Göring, and Joseph Goebbels, although he did not get along with the latter two and even offered to kill them.

Siegel's Hollywood success was also tied to his involvement in illegal rackets with the syndicate. He devised a plan to extort movie studios by taking over local trade unions and staging strikes, which would force studios to pay him off in order to resume production. He also borrowed significant sums of money from celebrities without any intention of paying them back, counting on the fact that they would not ask for repayment. In just one year in Hollywood, Siegel received over $400,000 in loans from movie stars.

According to Siegel, Atomite was a revolutionary new explosive that could detonate without any accompanying sound or flash. This substance piqued the interest of Benito Mussolini and the Axis powers, who expressed interest in purchasing it. Mussolini even provided Siegel with an advance of $40,000 to scale up the production of the explosive.

In 1939, Siegel arranged a demonstration of Atomite for Mussolini and Nazi leaders, including Joseph Goebbels and Hermann Göring. However, the explosive failed to detonate during the presentation, resulting in Mussolini demanding the return of his advance.

In 1939, Bugsy Siegel, along with Whitey Krakower, Frankie Carbo, and Albert Tannenbaum, murdered Harry "Big Greenie" Greenberg outside his apartment. Greenberg posed a threat as he was considering becoming a police informant, and the hit was ordered by Siegel's boss, Buchalter. Tannenbaum eventually confessed to the murder and agreed to testify against Siegel, leading to Siegel's implication in the crime. He was put on trial in September 1941, with the trial gaining notoriety due to Siegel's preferential treatment in jail, which included being granted leave for dental visits, having female visitors, and refusing to eat prison food.

Siegel hired attorney Jerry Giesler for his defense, and after the deaths of two state witnesses, no additional witnesses came forward. Despite Tannenbaum's testimony being dismissed, Siegel's reputation was damaged as newspapers revealed his past and referred to him by his nickname, "Bugsy." Siegel despised this moniker, preferring to be addressed as "Ben" or "Mr. Siegel."

In May 1944, Siegel was arrested for bookmaking but was acquitted again later that year thanks to testimony from George Raft and Mack Gray.

LAS VEGAS

I n 1946, Bugsy Siegel saw an opportunity to transform his public image and expand into legitimate businesses through a partnership with William R. Wilkerson's Flamingo Hotel. Siegel had previously explored the possibility of expanding operations in southern Nevada during the 1930s, providing illicit services to crews constructing the Boulder Dam. After Lansky handed over operations in Nevada to Siegel, he left for Hollywood and turned the operation over to his lieutenant, Sedway.

In the mid-1940s, Siegel began lining things up in Las Vegas while his lieutenants worked on securing all gambling in Los Angeles. In May 1946, Siegel decided to change his agreement with Wilkerson to give himself control of the Flamingo. He planned to supply the best gambling, food, and entertainment at reasonable prices, believing that this would attract both high rollers and vacationers willing to gamble significant amounts of money.

Wilkerson was eventually forced to sell all of his stakes in the Flamingo under the threat of death and went into hiding in Paris for a time. After this point, the Flamingo became syndicate-run and Siegel's vision for a legitimate business venture became a reality.

After taking control of the Flamingo Hotel, Bugsy Siegel went on a spending spree, demanding the finest building money could buy despite postwar shortages. As costs soared, his checks began to bounce, and by October 1946, the Flamingo's expenses had exceeded $4 million. The costs continued to rise, reaching over $6 million in 1947. However, by late November of that year, the construction was almost complete.

According to local observers, Siegel's "maniacal chest-puffing" set the standard for future generations of notable casino moguls. His violent reputation did not help his situation, and after boasting that he had personally killed some men, Siegel reassured his head contractor, Del Webb, that they "only kill each other." Although Bugsy Siegel had a violent reputation, some of his associates saw a different side of him. They described him as an intense but charitable person who even made donations to the Damon Runyon Cancer Fund. Lou Wiener Jr., Siegel's Las Vegas attorney, said that he was "very well-liked" and "good to people."

Despite problems with the Outfit's wire service clearing up in Nevada and Arizona, Bugsy Siegel refused to report business in California, announcing to his colleagues that he was running the California syndicate by himself and would return the loans in his "own good time." Despite his defiance, the mob bosses were patient with Siegel, recognizing his value to their organization.

The Flamingo Hotel opened on December 26, 1946, but only the casino, lounge, theater, and restaurant were finished. Although a handful of celebrities attended the opening, the luxury rooms that would have enticed guests to stay and gamble were not ready. As losses began to mount, Siegel became irate and verbally abusive, even throwing out at least one family. The gaming tables were $275,000 in the red, and the operation shut down in late January 1947.

After being granted a second chance, Siegel knuckled down and made renovations, hired a publicist, and obtained good press. The hotel reopened on March 1, 1947, with Lansky present, and began turning a profit. However, despite the success, the mob bosses above Siegel were running out of patience, and at age 41, Siegel had made a name for himself in the annals of organized crime and Las Vegas history.

ASSASSINATION

Even today, the identity of Benjamin "Bugsy" Siegel's killer remains a mystery. The notorious gangster was shot in Southern California on June 20, 1947, six months after his Flamingo hotel-casino on the Las Vegas Strip opened to disastrous results during a rare winter rainstorm. The resort closed in early 1947 but reopened as the Fabulous Flamingo by springtime, and it still operates at the same site under the same name, albeit with a modern hotel-casino structure.

Siegel's brutal death at his girlfriend Virginia Hill's rented home in Beverly Hills continues to spark speculation over who was responsible every year around the anniversary of the incident. Numerous theories have emerged over the years, but the mystery of the 41-year-old Brooklyn-born mobster's murder persists.

The identity of Bugsy Siegel's killer may still be up for debate, but the gruesome nature of his death scene 71 years ago is not. In their 1963 true crime book The Green Felt Jungle, authors Ed Reid and Ovid Demaris recounted the events that occurred on that fateful night in Beverly Hills. Other writers have since provided additional details to fill in the picture.

At 10:45 p.m., a sniper armed with a .30-caliber military carbine positioned the barrel on the crossbar of a rose-covered pagoda's latticework outside Siegel's girlfriend's pink Moorish mansion at 810 N. Linden Drive. The sniper then fired nine steel-jacketed slugs through a window, into the living room.

Bugsy Siegel was reading a Los Angeles Times newspaper he had picked up from a restaurant earlier when he was shot four times - twice in the head and twice in the torso - while sitting on a chintz-covered sofa with a table lamp illuminating his head. The drapes were open, and one headshot propelled an eye 15 feet away onto the tiled dining room floor.

Out of the five shots that missed, one destroyed a marble statue of Bacchus on a grand piano, and another punctured a painting of a nude holding a wineglass. Siegel's close friend and Hollywood business associate, Allen Smiley, who was an investor in the Flamingo, was seated on the sofa with Siegel but hit the floor as soon as the shooting began. Smiley's jacket was ripped by gunfire.

At the time of the shooting, Virginia Hill was not home. She had left for Paris after an argument with Siege a week earlier. The question remains: who was responsible for the shooting, and why?

Many people find the theory presented in the 1991 movie Bugsy, featuring Warren Beatty as Siegel and Annette Bening as Virginia Hill, to be plausible. In reality, those who knew Siegel referred to him as Ben, never "Bugsy." As former Las Vegas casino executive Bill Friedman noted in his book 30 Illegal Years to the Strip, the nickname "Bugsy" originated from something Siegel said as a child that the newspapers picked up on.

The movie, which was based on Dean Jennings' 1967 book We Only Kill Each Other, portrays a meeting in Havana, Cuba, where Mob leaders, including Siegel's childhood friend Meyer Lansky, express their anger over the Flamingo's construction overruns. As their money was at stake, they suspect that Virginia Hill may have been stealing cash from the project.

The 1991 movie Bugsy, starring Warren Beatty and Annette Bening, presented a premise that many people find convincing. In the film, based on the book We Only Kill Each Other by Dean Jennings, mob leaders including Meyer Lansky discuss cost overruns during the construction of the Flamingo in Havana, Cuba. Later, Siegel is shot multiple times by an unknown shooter firing from outside Virginia Hill's home. While the movie portrays the killing as taking place immediately after the Flamingo's grand opening, the actual event happened in June 1947. Nevertheless, the notion that the hit was ordered by the mob has gained traction beyond the screen. Although the shooter's identity remains unknown, some suspect New York killer John "Frankie" Carbo. Even former Philadelphia Mafia boss Ralph Natale believes that Lansky set up Siegel's assassination, which Carbo carried out.

In Ovid Demaris' 1980 book The Last Mafioso, West Coast hitman Jimmy "The Weasel" Fratianno, a former head of the Los Angeles crime family turned government witness, supports the theory that New York killer John "Frankie" Carbo was responsible for Siegel's murder, carrying out Lansky's orders. Fratianno claims that L.A. Mafia boss Jack Dragna told him about the hit, saying that Siegel's misuse of "important" people's money in constructing the Flamingo was the motive. Dragna warned Fratianno that messing with someone else's money was the quickest way to get killed.

Bernie Sindler, an emissary of Lansky's during the Flamingo's construction and a dissenting voice, refutes the theory of Siegel's murder being a Mob hit. In a 2017 interview with author Geoff Schumacher at The Mob Museum, Sindler, now in his 90s, argued that Siegel was "untouchable" because Charles "Lucky" Luciano, who was the head of everything, would have had to give permission for Siegel's killing. Since Lansky was close to Luciano, he would have never allowed the killing to happen, Sindler added.

Moreover, Sindler refuted the alleged financial motive for Siegel's killing, saying that Lansky paid back all Flamingo investors who wanted out, and by May 1947, after the hotel-casino had reopened, it raked in $10 million in four weeks.

This made Siegel "untouchable," according to Sindler. Additionally, Sindler pointed out that the method used to kill Siegel was not consistent with how the Mob typically carried out assassinations. The shooter fired from outside the house, which increases the risk of missing. Mob hit men usually opted for a shot to the back of the head from a killer sitting behind the victim in a car, reducing the risk of missing.

Sindler argued that the shooter was actually one of Virginia Hill's brothers, a U.S. Marine named either Bob or Bill. The brother in question was serving at Camp Pendleton, located near Oceanside, California.. Sindler claimed that he saw Virginia Hill and her military brother in front of the Flamingo, arguing about Siegel beating her up, about two weeks before the hotel-casino opened in late 1946.

The mystery surrounding Benjamin "Bugsy" Siegel's death persists, with various theories circulating to this day. Some speculate that the killing was related to a power struggle over control of the race wire in the West, while others suspect that Mob operatives from Chicago or Detroit were involved.

Despite the many theories, no one has ever been charged in Siegel's murder. Even his close friend and business associate, Allen Smiley, knew that people would continue to seek answers about the shooting.

In her memoir Cradle of Crime: A Daughter's Tribute, Luellen Smiley recounts a conversation with her father in the early 1980s when he was near the end of his life. At Cedars-Sinai Hospital in Los Angeles with a failing liver, Allen Smiley was asked about the Siegel killing. While he did not reveal any specific details, he acknowledged that he knew who was responsible for the shooting.

Despite numerous theories and speculation, the answer to the question, "Who killed Ben Siegel?" remains unknown.

FINAL LEGACY

Bugsy Siegel, a notorious gangster and one of the founders of Las Vegas, was a complex figure who defied easy characterization. His life was marked by violence, crime, and glamour, and his influence on American culture and history is still felt to this day. In this book, we have explored the life and legacy of Bugsy Siegel, examining his rise to power, his involvement in organized crime, and his role in the development of Las Vegas.

Siegel's life was marked by contradictions. He was a ruthless gangster who was also a charming socialite. He was a man who rose from poverty to wealth and power, but who remained driven by a desire for more. His vision of Las Vegas as a glamorous oasis in the desert transformed the city into the entertainment capital of the world, but his methods for achieving that vision were often illegal and immoral.

Despite his notoriety, Bugsy Siegel remains a

fascinating figure whose life is worth exploring. His story is a reminder of the dark side of the American Dream, and the ways in which crime, corruption, and violence have shaped the nation's history. But it is also a story of innovation, creativity, and daring, and of a man whose legacy continues to influence American culture and society.

In conclusion, Bugsy Siegel was a complex figure who defies easy characterization. He was a gangster, a visionary, a killer, and a charmer. He was both loved and hated, feared and admired. His legacy is still felt today in the city he helped create, and his story is a reminder of the enduring power of the American Dream, and the dark forces that sometimes accompany it.

MURDER INC

Murder, Inc. was a ruthless and highly organized group that acted as the muscle of the National Crime Syndicate during its reign from 1929 to 1941. The syndicate included several criminal organizations, such as the Italian-American Mafia, Jewish Mob, and others. The group was first led by Louis "Lepke" Buchalter and later by Albert "The Mad Hatter" Anastasia.

It is believed that Murder, Inc. was responsible for hundreds of contract killings, and their reign of terror continued until 1941 when former member Abe "Kid Twist" Reles turned informant, leading to the group's exposure. Following Reles' testimony, many members were convicted and executed, including Reles himself, who died under suspicious circumstances. The group's downfall was a significant victory for law enforcement in the battle against organized crime.

Thomas E. Dewey, who later became the 47th

governor of New York, gained notoriety as a prosecutor of Murder, Inc. and other organized crime cases. The group's legacy has left a lasting impact on the public perception of organized crime and the fight against it.

Murder, Inc. was composed of both Italian and Jewish gangsters, mainly recruited from poor and working-class neighborhoods such as the Lower East Side of Manhattan and Brooklyn's Brownsville, East New York, and Ocean Hill. They acted as enforcers for Jewish mobster Louis "Lepke" Buchalter, while also accepting murder contracts from mob bosses across the United States. Despite Mafia turncoat Joe Valachi's insistence that Murder, Inc. did not commit crimes for the Italian-American Mafia, other sources and the fact that Albert Anastasia was the head of an Italian-American Mafia crime family contradict this claim.

The group was based in part in Rosie "Midnight Rose" Gold's candy store at the corner of Saratoga and Livonia Ave in Brooklyn. They used a variety of weapons, including ice picks, to carry out their murders. Although the group had several members, Harry "Pittsburgh Phil" Strauss was the most prolific killer, with over 100 murders attributed to him (some historians place the number as high as 500).

Murder, Inc. hit men received a regular salary as well as an average fee of $1,000 to $5,000 per killing, with their families also receiving financial benefits.

PRELUDE TO MURDER INC

T he early 20th century saw the rise of numerous criminal gangs in New York City, with the Bugs and Meyer Mob being one of the most notable. Founded by Jewish American mobsters Meyer Lansky and Benjamin "Bugsy" Siegel in the 1920s, this gang was the precursor to Murder, Incorporated, a notorious organized crime group that would later become the enforcement arm of the National Crime Syndicate.

Following the Castellammarese War and the assassination of several "Mustache Petes," the Sicilian mob boss Charles "Lucky" Luciano formed the Commission and began collaborating closely with Lansky and the Jewish Mob, eventually leading to the formation of the National Crime Syndicate. In this multi-ethnic alliance, largely consisting of Italian and Jewish gangsters, the Bugs and Meyer gang was disbanded and replaced with Murder, Incorporated.

Operating from 1929 to 1941, Murder, Inc. was responsible for an estimated 400 to 1,000 contract killings before being exposed by former member Abe "Kid Twist" Reles. The subsequent trials resulted in numerous convictions and executions, and even Reles himself died under suspicious circumstances. Thomas E. Dewey, who gained prominence as a prosecutor of organized crime cases, including Murder, Inc., went on to become the governor of New York.

FOUNDATION

Murder, Inc. was established as a subsidiary of the National Crime Syndicate, and its operations were largely overseen by Louis "Lepke" Buchalter and Albert Anastasia, who was an underboss of the Mangano crime family. The group consisted of members from various criminal organizations, including Buchalter's labor-slugging gang and a group of enforcers from Brownsville, Brooklyn led by Martin "Buggsy" Goldstein and Abe "Kid Twist" Reles. The syndicate's board of directors, including Buchalter and occasionally Joe Adonis, provided the group with its orders. Albert "The Mad Hatter" Anastasia was the primary leader of the group, also known as the "Lord High Executioner", with support from Jacob "Gurrah" Shapiro, a longtime associate of Lepke.

In 1932, Abe Wagner became an informant and revealed information about the crime syndicate to the police. Fearing for his safety, Wagner fled to Saint Paul, Minnesota, and disguised himself to avoid detection. However, two members of Murder, Inc., George Young and Joseph Schafer, tracked him down and fatally shot him. They were later captured, and Bugsy Siegel's efforts to have them released were unsuccessful.

During the 1930s, Louis Buchalter used Murder, Inc. to eliminate witnesses and suspected informants while being investigated by prosecutor Thomas Dewey. In one particularly gruesome incident on May 11, 1937, four hitmen brutally murdered loan shark George Rudnick based solely on suspicions that he was an informant. On October 1, 1937, they shot and severely injured Max Rubin, a former associate of Buchalter who had refused to follow orders to leave town and avoid testifying against him. The group was also responsible for the deaths of Morris Kessler and brothers Louis and Joseph Amberg in 1935.

DUTCH SHULTZ ASSASSINATION

I n the 1930s, Murder, Inc.'s most high-profile target was Dutch Schultz, a mobster who had openly challenged the syndicate's authority. In October 1935, Schultz defied the syndicate board by insisting on putting a hit on crusading prosecutor Thomas Dewey, who was leading an aggressive campaign to dismantle organized crime. The board feared that Dewey's assassination would lead to a public outcry and increased pressure to crack down on the mob. Despite their objections, Schultz threatened to kill Dewey himself.

To prevent Schultz from carrying out his plan, the syndicate board decided to eliminate him first. This decision ultimately saved Dewey's life and allowed him to continue his efforts to bring down the mob. Louis Buchalter, head of Murder, Inc., played a key role in the plot to kill Schultz. Despite his reputation as a ruthless killer, some have argued that Buchalter's actions actually helped to uphold the rule of law by thwarting Schultz's attempt on Dewey's life. In hindsight, some members of the syndicate have suggested that Schultz should have been allowed to carry out his plan, but at the time, the board stood firm in their decision to eliminate him.

Mendy Weiss and Charles Workman were hired by the syndicate to eliminate Dutch Schultz, who had become a liability to the organization. On October 24, 1935, Weiss and Workman ambushed Schultz and his associates at the Palace Chop House in Newark, New Jersey, killing Otto Berman, Abe Landau, and Lulu Rosenkrantz. Although Schultz survived the initial attack, he died the following day from his wounds. Workman stayed behind to ensure the job was completed, while Weiss fled the scene with the getaway driver Seymour Schechter.

Feeling betrayed, Workman filed a complaint with the syndicate against Weiss and Schechter. Although Schechter had simply followed Weiss's orders to leave without waiting for Workman, he was punished nonetheless, becoming a victim of Murder, Inc. himself shortly thereafter. Weiss was later executed for another murder, and Workman was eventually sentenced to 23 years in prison for his role in the Schultz assassination.

DOWNFALL

I n January 1940, Harry Rudolph, a professional criminal and police informant, was detained as a material witness in the murder of minor gangster Alex Alpert, who was shot in the back on a street corner in Brooklyn's Brownsville section in November 1933. While in custody, Rudolph spoke with Brooklyn District Attorney William O'Dwyer and provided testimony that led to the indictment of Abe Reles, Martin Goldstein, and Anthony Maffetore on charges of first-degree murder.

However, it was later discovered that Rudolph had been offered a bribe of $5,000 by another prisoner, acting on behalf of the syndicate, to retract his testimony and clear Reles and Goldstein. Maffetore learned of this offer and, after several conversations with New York City Detective John Osnato, decided to turn state's evidence, leading to further revelations about the criminal activities of the syndicate.

Maffetore eventually decided to cooperate with the District Attorney's office and admitted to being the driver in six gangland murders, including the murder of Alpert. He then convinced Abraham Levine to talk, and Reles followed suit, leading to numerous first-degree murder indictments across Brooklyn, the Bronx, and upstate Sullivan County. Other members of the "Combination" also became cooperating witnesses, including Tannenbaum, Magoon, and Bernstein. Harry Rudolph's testimony was never used in any of the trials, as he passed away from natural causes while in custody at Rikers Island in June 1940.

However, Reles met a mysterious death when he fell from a room at the Half Moon Hotel in Coney Island on November 12, 1941, despite being under police guard. Although the official verdict was an accidental death, many have speculated that Reles was murdered to prevent him from testifying against other members of the National Crime Syndicate.

THE TRIALS

Trial 1

Harry Maione and Frank Abbandando, members of the Brooklyn "Combination," were the first to stand trial for murder. Their trial began in May 1940 for the murder of George "Whitey" Rudnick on May 25, 1937, in a Brooklyn parking garage. Harry Strauss was also charged with the murder but was separated from the trial after initially agreeing to cooperate with the District Attorney's office. According to Abe Reles' testimony on May 15, 1940, Harry Strauss alleged that George Rudnick was providing information to the police, and as a result, Rudnick was targeted for assassination. Reles stated that he waited outside the garage while Maione, Abbandando, and Strauss were inside with Rudnick. Following the belief that Rudnick was murdered, Abbandando called for Reles and requested Angelo "Julie" Catalano's assistance in relocating the body. Despite Rudnick still being alive, Strauss continued to attack him with an ice pick, and Maione utilized a meat cleaver to complete the killing. The next day, Catalano corroborated Reles' account of the murder. "Dukey" Maffetore and Abe "Pretty" Levine testified that they stole the car used to dispose of the body. Maione claimed that he was at his grandmother's wake during the time of Rudnick's murder, and he had the support of 14 witnesses who testified to his alibi. However, the undertaker and embalmer at the funeral home testified that Maione was not present at the wake, contradicting his claim. Additionally, one of Maione's key witnesses admitted to committing perjury as ordered by Maione's brother, whom he feared.

On May 23, 1940, Maione and Abbandando were found guilty of first-degree murder, which carried a mandatory death sentence by electric chair. In December 1940, the Court of Appeals, the highest court in New York, overturned the conviction with a 4-3 vote. The second trial began on March 10, 1941, during which Maione threw a glass of water at Reles in anger. On April 3, 1941, Maione and Abbandando were convicted of first-degree murder for the second time and formally sentenced to death on April 14, 1941. The second conviction of Maione and Abbandando was affirmed by the Court of Appeals on January 8, 1942, and they were subsequently executed at Sing Sing prison on February 19, 1942.

Trial 2

Harry Strauss and Martin Goldstein were brought to trial for the murder of bookmaker Irving Feinstein on September 4, 1939. The victim's body had been set on fire and left in a vacant lot after he was strangled. During the trial, Strauss pretended to be insane while Reles, the prosecution's main witness, claimed that the murder was ordered by Albert Anastasia, as Feinstein had crossed Vincent Mangano. Reles testified that he, Strauss, and Goldstein committed the murder in the victim's house. Goldstein's former bodyguard/driver, Seymour Magoon, also testified to the same. Strauss's lawyer claimed that he was insane, and he was briefly allowed on the witness stand but refused to take his oath and began babbling incoherently. On September 19, 1940, Strauss and Goldstein were found guilty of first-degree murder, and one week later, they were sentenced to death. In April 1941, their convictions were affirmed by New York's Court of Appeals on a 4-3 decision, and Strauss and Goldstein were executed in the electric chair on June 12, 1941.

Trial 3

Charles Workman was accused and indicted for the murder of Dutch Schultz and three other members of his gang in October 1935, and was extradited to New Jersey in April 1941. The trial began in June 1941 and featured testimony from Abe Reles and Albert Tannenbaum, who were the primary underworld witnesses against Workman. The trial started with two state witnesses failing to identify Workman, but Reles and Tannenbaum later provided their testimony implicating him. During the trial, a woman who was a friend of Danny Fields and involved in collecting payrolls for Lepke testified that Workman came to her apartment the day after Schultz's murder and spoke candidly about the killing. Marty Krompier, a close associate of Dutch Schultz who was shot in Manhattan on the same night as Schultz's murder in New Jersey, testified as the first witness for Workman's defense.. Workman changed his plea to 'no contest' after one of his chief defense witnesses recanted his testimony that had provided Workman with an alibi. Workman was sentenced to life in prison on the same day he changed his plea. On March 10, 1964, he was released on parole after spending 23 years in prison.

Trial 4

Irving Nitzberg, a member of the Brooklyn "Combination," was tried for the murder of Albert Shuman in Brooklyn in January 1939. The prosecution's case relied on the testimonies of Abe Reles, Albert Tannenbaum, and Seymour Magoon, who stated that Nitzberg had killed Shuman because he had cooperated with the authorities investigating Lepke's involvement in labor racketeering. Reles testified that he helped plan the murder with Lepke, Mendy Weiss, and Albert Anastasia, who had approved the use of someone living outside Brooklyn to carry out the killing. Tannenbaum testified that he drove Nitzberg and Shuman under the pretext of a robbery, and Nitzberg shot Shuman twice in the back of the head when Tannenbaum gave the signal. Nitzberg was convicted of first-degree murder and sentenced to death in the electric chair in May 1941, but the conviction was overturned on December 10, 1941, on a 4-3 vote by the Court of Appeals, which raised questions about the use of non-accomplice witness testimony. Nitzberg was tried a second time in 1942, but the conviction was again overturned by the Court of Appeals on a 4-3 vote, and the indictment was dismissed due to the lack of corroborating testimony from non-accomplice witnesses before the Grand Jury.

Trial 5

Louis Buchalter, Emanuel Weiss, Louis Capone, Harry Strauss, and James Feraco were indicted for the murder of Brooklyn trucking executive Joseph Rosen. However, Cohen's murder indictment was dropped before the trial started due to his conviction on a federal narcotics charge. Feraco was presumed killed in 1940 or 1941, and Strauss had already been executed for another murder. The trial faced difficulty in securing a jury for Lepke. It finally began in October 1941 after jury selection in August that year. The trial featured the testimony of Rosen's wife and son, a teacher, and underworld informant Sholem Bernstein, who had refused to carry out a murder contract and was marked for death. Capone, Lepke, and Weiss, were convicted on November 30, 1941. The Court of Appeals upheld their murder convictions in October 1942, and the US Supreme Court refused to hear Lepke's appeal in February 1943. However, in March 1943, the Supreme Court granted a review to Lepke, Weiss, and Capone. In June 1943 The Supreme Court upheld the conviction. Before Lepke's execution, the federal government needed to transfer him to New York State's custody, as he was serving a 14-year sentence in federal prison. Lepke continued to appeal his death sentence vigorously, but he, Weiss, and Capone were eventually executed in Sing-Sing prison on March 4, 1944.

Trial 6

Vito "Socko" Gurino was wanted for questioning in a murder investigation involving the Brooklyn "Combination" due to his role in eliminating witnesses. Gurino attempted to silence a gangster who witnessed the murder of George Rudnick and then tried to convince another gang member to "hide out" on Long Island. Later, Gurino used a corrupt deputy sheriff to force a material witness, Joseph "Joe the Baker" Liberto, to meet with him in prison and threatened him with death if he cooperated with the District Attorney. Gurino was arrested in September 1940 at a church in Manhattan and confessed to multiple syndicate murders. He pleaded guilty to three murders in March 1942 and was sentenced to 80 years to life in prison. Gurino passed away due to a heart ailment at the Dannemora Hospital for the Criminally Insane on April 22, 1957.

Trial 7

Jacob Drucker and Irving Cohen faced separate trials for the murder of racketeer Walter Sage in the Catskills. Sage was killed with an ice pick and had a slot machine frame tied to his body when it was found in Swan Lake on July 31, 1937. After the murder, Cohen fled to California, fearing for his life, and found work as an extra in films. Two years later, he was identified by Abraham Levine, the chief prosecution witness, who saw Cohen in a crowd scene in the 1939 film Golden Boy. Levine testified that Cohen and Drucker were in the car with Sage when he was stabbed 32 times with an ice pick. Drucker also stabbed Cohen once in the arm during the struggle. Cohen testified that Levine and another man assaulted him with an ice pick, claiming that it was on Drucker's orders because he refused to pay a 25% profit on a game of chance he operated. Cohen was acquitted on June 21, 1940, but Drucker, who was a suspect in four Catskills murders, remained a fugitive until the FBI located him in Delaware. Drucker was convicted of second-degree murder on May 5, 1944, and sentenced to 25 years to life. He died in Attica prison in January 1962.

Trial 8

Jack "the Dandy" Parisi was charged with the murders of Morris Diamond and Irving Penn, the latter of which was a case of mistaken identity. Parisi evaded authorities for a decade until he was captured in Pennsylvania in 1949. The prosecution called on Albert Tannenbaum, who was living in Atlanta, to testify against Parisi. One of Parisi's accomplices in the Penn murder, Jacob "Kuppy" Migden, pleaded guilty to attempted first-degree assault and was sentenced to 5-10 years in prison. Parisi was acquitted of both murders in separate trials as the judges directed a verdict of not guilty due to a lack of corroborating evidence, as the key witnesses were accomplices. Parisi died of natural causes at the age of 83 at his home on December 27, 1982.

AL CAPONE: THE RISE, REIGN, AND FALL OF THE NOTORIOUS GANGSTER AL CAPONE (PROHIBITION AND ORGANIZED CRIME)

By Patrick Auerbach

Here is a preview of another book you may enjoy.

I. INTRODUCTION

Alphonse Gabriel Capone, also known as "Scarface," was a notorious American gangster and crime boss who rose to power during the Prohibition era in the 1920s. Capone became involved in organized crime at a young age and eventually rose to prominence in a criminal empire based in Chicago. Capone's notoriety and infamy reached a peak in the late 1920s and early 1930s when he became a symbol of the corruption and lawlessness that plagued America during the Prohibition era. Born in Brooklyn, New York on January 17, 1899, Capone grew up in a rough neighborhood and became involved in petty crime and gang activity at a young age. By the early 1920s, he had risen the ladder to become the leader of a vast criminal empire (based in Chicago).

During the Prohibition era, Capone's illegal activities included bootlegging, gambling, prostitution, and racketeering. He controlled a vast network of illegal enterprises, and his influence extended throughout the city of Chicago and beyond. Capone was known for his brutal methods and his ruthless tactics.

Despite numerous attempts by law enforcement to bring him to justice, Capone managed to evade conviction for many years. He was finally arrested and convicted of tax evasion in 1931, and he spent the last years of his life in federal prison. He died of a heart attack on January 25, 1947, but his legacy lives on as one of the most notorious and colorful figures in American history.

II. EARLY LIFE AND RISE TO POWER

T his chapter explores Capone's early life, including his childhood and family background, and provides insight into the family dynamics that shaped him. The chapter sheds light on the events and experiences that influenced Capone's development and laid the foundation for his later criminal activities.

Al Capone's upbringing and early life played a significant role in shaping the man he would become. Born in Brooklyn, New York in 1899, Capone grew up in a rough neighborhood and was exposed to crime and violence at a young age. Despite this, his family life was filled with love and support.

Capone was the fourth of nine children born to Italian immigrants Gabriele and Teresina Capone. His father was a barber, while his mother stayed at home to care for the children. Capone's childhood was marked by poverty, and he dropped out of school at the age of 14 to help support his family.

Despite the challenges he faced, Capone remained close to his family throughout his life. He was especially close to his mother, who doted on him and often referred to him as "my baby." Capone was also close to his siblings, and he maintained close relationships with them throughout his life.

ENTRY INTO ORGANIZED CRIME

Now we will look at Capone's entry into organized crime, including his association with the Five Points Gang and his rise to prominence under Johnny Torrio. The chapter sets the stage for a deeper exploration of Capone's criminal activities and his rise to power in the Prohibition era.

Al Capone's entry into organized crime marked a turning point in his life and set him on a path to becoming one of the most notorious gangsters in American history. After dropping out of school at the age of 14, Capone became involved in petty crime and gang activity in Brooklyn, New York.

It was in these early years that Capone became associated with the notorious Five Points Gang, a criminal organization that dominated the underworld of New York City. Johnny Torrio was a notorious street gang leader and among his members was Lucky Luciano, who would later become famous in his own right. Capone quickly rose through the ranks, displaying a natural talent for violence and an unquenchable thirst for power.

In 1919, Capone moved to Chicago to again work for the notorious gangster Johnny Torrio. Under Torrio's guidance, Capone gained valuable experience in the world of organized crime and rose to prominence as a key figure in the Chicago underworld.

Amazon US: https://www.amazon.com/dp/BOBTZRPHMD

Amazon UK: https://www.amazon.co.uk/dp/BOBTZRPHMD

WORKS CITED

"Benjamin "Bugsy" Siegel." *The Mob Museum*, https://themobmuseum.org/notable_names/ benjamin-bugsy-siegel/. Accessed March 2023.

Buchalter, Louis, and Albert Anastasia. "Lucky Luciano | Biography & Facts | Britannica." *Encyclopedia Britannica*, 22 January 2023, https://www.britannica.com/biography/ Lucky-Luciano. Accessed February 2023.

Carpozi Jr., George, and William Balsamo. *The Mafia: The First 100 Years*. Ebury Publishing, 2019.

"Castellammarese War." *Wikipedia*, https:// en.wikipedia.org/wiki/Castellammarese_War.

Accessed February 2023.

Cawthorne, Nigel. *The Mammoth Book of the Mafia*. Edited by Nigel Cawthorne and Colin Cawthorne, Robinson, 2009.

Editors, Charles River. "Bugsy Siegel and Meyer Lansky: The Controversial Mobsters Who Worked with Lucky Luciano to Form the National Crime Syndicate." *Amazon UK*, https://www.amazon.co.uk/Bugsy-Siegel-Meyer-Lansky-Controversial-ebook/dp/B07LC22YBB/ref=d_reads_cwrtbar_sccl_1_3/262-5039638-0669035?pd_rd_w=qgJw5&content-id=amzn1.sym.b16e386e-23e7-4b41-a80e-3d3c8ef235f9&pf_rd_p=b16e386e-23e7-4b41-a80e-3d3c8ef235f9&pf_rd. Accessed March 2023.

"Ep 6: Living to Serve | SEARCH ON." *YouTube*, 12 June 2018, https://

darksideoflife.blog/2022/04/12/head-of-the-commission-the-rise-of-charles-lucky-luciano. Accessed February 2023.

Henry, Larry. "Who killed Benjamin "Bugsy" Siegel?" *The Mob Museum*, 25 May 2018, https://themobmuseum.org/blog/killed-benjamin-bugsy-siegel/. Accessed March 2023.

"Lucky Luciano - Death, Life & Crimes." *bio. Biography.com*, 2 April 2014, https://www.biography.com/crime/lucky-luciano. Accessed February 2023.

"Lucky Luciano Lucky Luciano." *Timenote*, https://timenote.info/en/Lucky-Luciano. Accessed February 2023.

Raab, Selwyn. *Five Families: The Rise, Decline, and Resurgence of America's Most Powerful Mafia Empires*. St. Martin's Press, 2006.

Scaduto, Anthony. *Lucky Luciano: The Man who*

Modernized the Mafia. Sphere, 1976.

Silver, Carly. "Lucky Luciano: The Real-Life Godfather Who Invented The Mafia As We Know It." *All That's Interesting*, 3 September 2022, https://allthatsinteresting.com/lucky-luciano. Accessed February 2023.

FREE BOOKS

Sign up for my newsletter for free Kindle books. By joining my newsletter, you will be notified when my books are free on Amazon so you can download them and not have to pay!

You will also be notified when I release a new book and be able to buy it for a reduced price.

You will also get a free Spartans and the Battle of Thermopylae book delivered to your inbox (in PDF format) that can be read on your laptop, phone, or tablet.

Finally, you will receive free history articles delivered to your inbox once a week.

Simply click the link below to sign up and receive your free book:

https://mailchi.mp/2ebbbf6b6a7f/history-newsletter